Stylin'

Great Looks
for Teens

Maggie Marron

Stylin'

Great Looks
for Teens

Maggie Marron

FRIEDMAN/FAIRFAX

PUBLISHERS

A FRIEDMAN/FAIRFAX BOOK

Please visit our website: www.metrobooks.com

© 2001 by Michael Friedman Publishing Group, Inc.

Library of Congress Cataloging-in-Publication Data
available upon request.

ISBN 1-58663-079-2

Editor: Ann Kirby
Art Director: Jeff Batzli
Designer: Midori Nakamura
Photo Editor: Jami Ruszkai
Production Manager: Rosy Ngo

Color separations by Fine Arts Repro House Co., Ltd.
Printed in China by Lee Fung–Asco Printers Ltd.

3 5 7 9 10 8 6 4 2

Distributed by Sterling Publishing Company, Inc.
387 Park Avenue South
New York, NY 10016
Distributed in Canada by Sterling Publishing
Canadian Manda Group
One Atlantic Avenue, Suite 105
Toronto, Ontario, Canada M6K 3E7
Distributed in Australia by
Capricorn Link (Australia) Pty Ltd.
P.O. Box 704
Windsor, NSW 2756 Australia

Dedication

For **Carl J.** and **Randy D.**,
the stylin'est babes I know!

Thanks to the usual suspects
who helped make this book a success,
especially to **Christine Guarino Mayer**,
who helped dig up many of these juicy tips
and provided expert advice on makeup,
and **Maria Tahim** for her fab suggestions
and shoe wisdom.
Thanks also to **Ann Kirby-Payne**,
my wonderful editor,
for letting me take a stab at this project.
Last but not least, thanks to **Francine Hornberger**
for being such a style maven!

Contents

Introduction

How do you define style? Is it all about hair? Makeup? Fashion? Some combination of the three? There's no simple answer—style is different for everyone, and it's something that everyone has. Some girls follow fashion the way men follow football, and will settle for nothing less than wearing the latest trends; others are a lot more comfortable in the classics, whether clean A-line dresses or tried-and-true blue jeans. Some like to glam up with lots of makeup, while others prefer a more natural look. Some accessorize with fun dangling earrings, others settle for simple gold or jeweled studs. Each choice you make helps lay the foundation for your own unique style, and worn the right way, each of these options is equally stylish. But style isn't always about what you choose to wear; often, it's more about how you wear it. Clothes, hair, makeup, and accessories are only part of the package—it takes a touch of attitude and a good dose of sensibility to create your own style.

In all the time I've been profiling celebrities, I've found there's one thing they all have in common: to be a star, they've had to cultivate their own unique style. Style is what separates Christina Aguilera from Britney Spears, Alyssa Milano from Angelina Jolie. Each of these celebs has created her own look, and her style choices are what stick with the audience's memory after the movie, video, or concert ends.

I put this book together to help you find your own style by taking a close look at how some of your favorite celebs use fashion, makeup, hair, and accessories. A little Jennifer Lopez here, a little Mandy Moore there, a little Gwen Stefani thrown in for good measure. Use this book to check out what your favorite glam gals are doing—and as an inspiration to create a style of your very own!

And I mean that. When you set out to find your own sense of style, don't copy anyone else outright. Don't wear everything Brandy wears because you soooo love her. Take inspiration from friends, celebrities, stylish people you see on the street, and then pick and choose to make your own look. And that doesn't mean having the same style all the time. You can have lots of fun being a fashion chameleon—just do it well. As you'll learn in this book, style is about so much more than imitation—it's about originality, expression, comfort, and just plain fun! Enjoy!

—Maggie

Stylin' Head 2 Toe

Perfectly groomed brows, earth-toned shadow, and dark liner add definition to Lacey's warm brown eyes. A coat of mascara gives even more emphasis to her naturally luscious lashes. A coat of rosy-brown matte lipstick is the finishing touch.

Lacey's naturally brown locks are worn straight, but not pin straight—she hasn't spent hours with a straightening iron. Falling to her shoulders with just enough styling products to give it body, shine, and control, her hair looks perfect without looking "done."

Hair, make-up, clothes, accessories... when it comes to style, the whole look is often more than just the sum of its parts. Here are a few different looks modeled by celebs who know how to pull it all together.

Ask any fashion consultant to name the most classic piece of clothing, the one item that no woman should be without, and they'll tell you it's a little black dress. Lacey opts for a simple street-length sheath with spaghetti straps and a hint of illusion at the neckline.

Glitz is kept to a bare minimum, with a simple floating diamond pendant and a silver ring.

A pair of dark shades, the ultimate accessory for anyone.

Classic

Lacey Chabert will never look back at what she wore to the Fox network bash and wonder what she was thinking. Everything from her hair to her hemline is the epitome of classic. The entire outfit would work on just about anyone, yet it makes a unique fashion statement: the look is smart, sophisticated, and timeless, and tells people that she's all those things, too.

Strappy black platform sandals complete the look, making this a simple yet striking summer outfit. Switch to a pair of black pumps, add a black pashmina, and Lacey could just as easily wear this dress to a winter event.

Letting her mane of gorgeous honey-gold hair fall free is a statement in itself about the earthy, playful mood Mandy's in today.

When it comes to her makeup, Mandy usually opts for the natural look. Even with a groovy ensemble like this one, simple pale neutrals are all this Neutrogena spokesmodel needs on her fresh face.

Mandy punctuates her look with a pair of long, beaded earrings falling around her neck.

Mandy pairs a funky feathered halter with a fringed denim skirt for an ensemble that is pure haute couture.

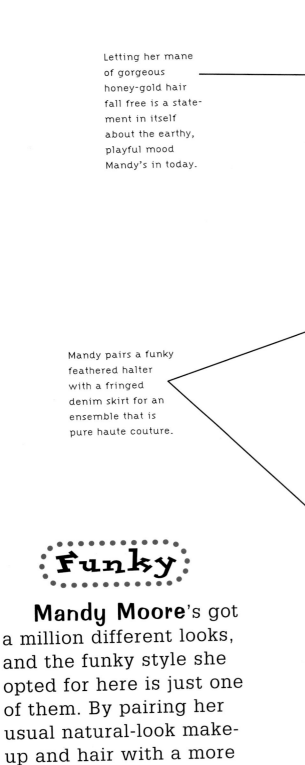

Matching feathered sandals pull the whole package together.

Funky

Mandy Moore's got a million different looks, and the funky style she opted for here is just one of them. By pairing her usual natural-look makeup and hair with a more off-the-wall outfit, Mandy creates a unique look that works as well in the real world as it does on the runway.

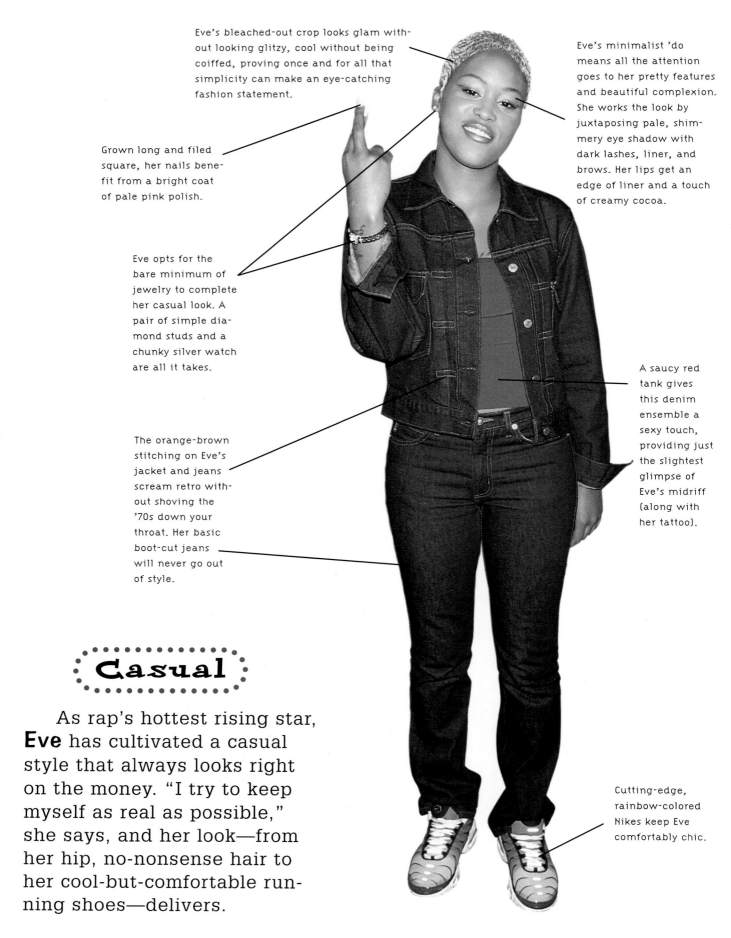

Eve's bleached-out crop looks glam without looking glitzy, cool without being coiffed, proving once and for all that simplicity can make an eye-catching fashion statement.

Eve's minimalist 'do means all the attention goes to her pretty features and beautiful complexion. She works the look by juxtaposing pale, shimmery eye shadow with dark lashes, liner, and brows. Her lips get an edge of liner and a touch of creamy cocoa.

Grown long and filed square, her nails benefit from a bright coat of pale pink polish.

Eve opts for the bare minimum of jewelry to complete her casual look. A pair of simple diamond studs and a chunky silver watch are all it takes.

A saucy red tank gives this denim ensemble a sexy touch, providing just the slightest glimpse of Eve's midriff (along with her tattoo).

The orange-brown stitching on Eve's jacket and jeans scream retro without shoving the '70s down your throat. Her basic boot-cut jeans will never go out of style.

Casual

As rap's hottest rising star, **Eve** has cultivated a casual style that always looks right on the money. "I try to keep myself as real as possible," she says, and her look—from her hip, no-nonsense hair to her cool-but-comfortable running shoes—delivers.

Cutting-edge, rainbow-colored Nikes keep Eve comfortably chic.

Britney blew out any natural waves to create a sleek, straight 'do, contributing to an elegant yet fresh and flirtatious look. For a more sophisticated feel, she might have chosen to wear her hair in a glamorous updo.

Britney usually opts for neutral shades that complement her tawny complexion and brown eyes. Here, she dresses up her usual look with shimmery pastel eye shadow and glossy, taupe lipstick.

A simple diamond solitaire on a platinum chain is all the adornment this stunning gown requires.

A floor-length gown of lavender organza looks sophisticated yet sweet: empire-waisted, with a beaded bodice, spaghetti straps, and a tiny train.

A cream colored pashmina keeps out the winter chill and adds a little drama to the otherwise simple silhouette.

Formal

Your most special events call for your most special outfits, and even woman-of-a-thousand-looks **Britney Spears** usually makes formal occasions an excuse to go pretty and fancy. The demure look she fashioned for the 1999 *Billboard* Awards says more about Britney's real style than any of the looks she's created on stage or in her videos.

With a long dress, you can pay less attention to shoes than you might otherwise, but it's important to make sure that when your toes peek out, they don't *stick* out. Britney wears a pair of lavender open-toed sandals to complete her formal look.

Chapter 1 ♥ Make-up Matters

♥
♥ ♥

From glitter-glam to nearly nude, the way you dress your face says a lot about who you are—or at least who you are TODAY.

Supermodel **Tyra Banks** wears layers of smoky gray shadow and jet black mascara to enhance her doe-like eyes. A dusting of iridescent powder gives her smooth skin a bit of runway-worthy sparkle.

The great thing about makeup is that you can change your look according to the **situation** (school versus work versus date, for instance), your **mood** (feeling sporty, or maybe a bit more daring?), even the **time of day**. And of course, you've got to take your **personality** into account—after all, no matter what kind of look you're going for, **it's still got to be you**.

Use makeup to enhance yourself, not to re-create yourself.

As a general rule, you should **keep daytime makeup soft and natural looking**. Too much makeup—or even worse, the wrong makeup—will only detract from your natural beauty. Think about Katie Holmes's natural, girl-next-door look: always fresh, clean, and real looking. At **night**, you might go for something a bit more **vampy**—consider a splash of deep red lipstick, or some wild blue eye shadow. Always pay attention to your natural coloring—your skin tone, your eye color, your hair.

This chapter will give you tips for choosing colors and shades that will work for you, and using them the right way.

A great place to start is with your own coloring. Earth tones, for example, look great on brown-eyed girls, while pastel shades complement pale eyes. If you're not sure about color, go to the makeup counter of a local department store—or even to your own salon if they offer makeup services—and have a color evaluation done. These evaluations are usually free, although the salespeople will try hard to get you to buy their products. Keep in mind that the most expensive brand is not necessarily the best—cosmetics sold in drugstores can be the same quality as pricier lines sold only in salons or department stores. So don't believe the hype—experiment, and find the brands that work best for you.

Laying a Perfect ♥ Foundation ♥

Just like building a house, you can't build a successful look without laying the proper foundation. In makeup terms—just like in building terms—you have to start with a solid foundation.

For a flawless complexion like **Natalie Portman**'s, match your foundation to the skin on your neck. Unless your skin is very dry, use a water-based formula, and choose a satin finish to complement your skin. A final dusting of powder keeps shine at bay and makeup in place.

Foundation is used to even out your skin tone and cover any imperfections. An added plus of foundation is that many brands include a **sunscreen** to shield your skin from damaging UV rays. If you've got great skin, you may not want or need to wear foundation, but remember that you really should use a moisturizer with an added sunscreen to keep your skin looking great for years to come.

For those of us who aren't blessed with perfect skin, here are some foundation pointers:

♥ ### The first step is to use a concealer to hide any blemishes or dark circles.

Choose a shade that matches your skin tone exactly—or even one that's slightly lighter than your skin tone. Don't try something darker or you'll draw attention to your flaws. Work your concealer in. It should disappear once applied.

♥ ### When you choose your foundation, be sure to pick one that matches your skin tone.

Try to match it to the skin on your neck rather than your cheeks, to avoid a nasty line around the border of your face. Never try to use foundation to make your skin lighter or darker than it is—if you do, you'll see the foundation instead of your skin, and you'll look like you're wearing a mask!

♥ ### Here's how to apply your foundation.

If you use an applicator sponge, dampen it first with water before putting the foundation on it to give it a more sheer look. If you're using your fingers, dab the foundation on one of your middle fingers and gently work it into the other. Apply foundation with these two fingers. Why? You'll be applying less pressure to your face and you'll get more even results. Be sure to blend the foundation onto your jawline and neck to avoid the "mask" look.

If liquid foundation seems too heavy for you, try a light dusting of translucent powder over your concealer for a fresh, natural look. Just make sure your skin tones are even enough for this light treatment.

Blushing Beauties

After you apply your foundation, you'll move on to your **blush**. When choosing a shade of blush, remember that **if it appears obvious when applied, it is not the right shade for you**. Blush should give your face a natural glow—it should never look like makeup at all.

Which shade is right for you?

Skin Tone	Blush Shade
Pale	Pastels; avoid brown
Light	Pale pinks or peach
Medium	Sandy pinks
Dark/Black	Plum or deep bronze
Yellow/Olive	Pink or rose; avoid peach or bronze

Is **Lisa Ling** wearing blush, or is that just her natural glow? Whether you're going for a casual day look or a more dramatic evening effect, properly applied blush looks totally natural.

Tips for applying blush:

♥ Use a round blush brush to apply blush to the apple of your cheeks—that's the part that pops up when you smile.

♥ Start from the center of your cheek and brush it on in an upward inverted "C" motion.

♥ Blend any harsh edges.

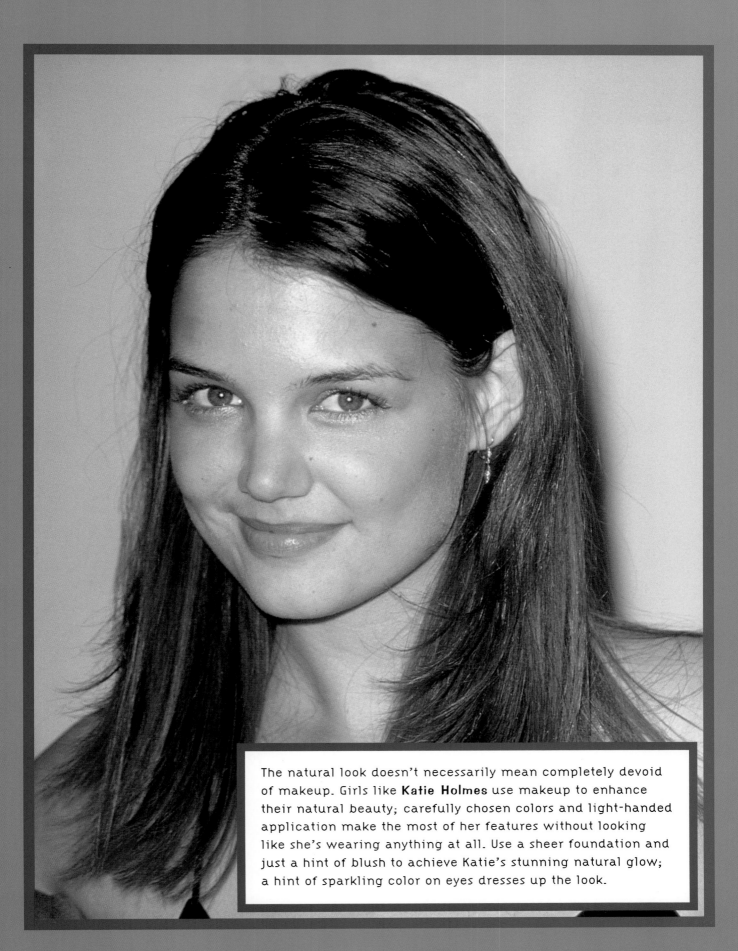

The natural look doesn't necessarily mean completely devoid of makeup. Girls like **Katie Holmes** use makeup to enhance their natural beauty; carefully chosen colors and light-handed application make the most of her features without looking like she's wearing anything at all. Use a sheer foundation and just a hint of blush to achieve Katie's stunning natural glow; a hint of sparkling color on eyes dresses up the look.

Eyes

In terms of make-up, nothing's more complicated than your eyes— or as important!

Ask any guy—okay, just about any guy—to name the first thing he notices about a girl, and nine out of ten times, you can be sure he'll say "her eyes." And in terms of style, the way you wear eye makeup says a lot about you. Your eyes make a big impression on people, so you really want to get them right. You don't want to look like a raccoon!

There are **four parts** to your eye makeup regimen. You may choose not to get into all of these—perhaps you're comfortable with eyeliner and mascara only, or maybe you prefer to use eye shadow for liner for a soft-er effect. **It's all about what you want—your own sense of style!**

Monica's pretty eye makeup looks gorgeous without going overboard. The trick is choosing a neutral shade that complements your skin tone to cover the whole lid, while a lighter shade accentuates the browbone. Adding a dash of sparkly pink shadow on the lids dresses up the look, while a touch of mascara and a bit of dark liner help define the eyes.

1. Eyeliner

Choose a shade that complements your natural colorings. Try to create a soft, subtle look—hard, edgy eyeliner is a thing of the past. Use your eyeliner to define your eye shape and make your lashes look thicker, fuller, and longer. You can choose a soft pencil, a liquid, or a perfect shade of eye shadow applied with a fine, damp brush.

2. Eye Shadow

There are so many different shades of eye shadow, as well as ways to apply these shades, that **you really have to pay attention to what suits you**. You can use eye shadow on your eyelid, but also under your eye, instead of—or along with—eyeliner. A pale shade over the entire lid and browbone paired with a darker color along the lash line and in the crease creates a dramatic yet simple look. After applying, use an eye shadow blender brush to blend the colors together and get rid of any harsh edges. **You want to emphasize your eyes, not overemphasize them.**

Keep in mind that while eye shadow is intended to highlight your eyes, it should match your skin tone, not your irises!

Here are a few suggestions:

♥ **For fair skin,**

try sand or beige for your eyelid and a pale green for your lash line.

♥ **For medium skin,**

try amber for your eyelid and an olive green for your lash line.

♥ **For dark skin,**

try taupe for your eyelid and cobalt blue for your lash line.

Of course, special occasions might call for a more glamorous look. **Bai Ling**'s delicate eyes steal the show when they are shadowed in stunning shades of gray and white. Notice how she pairs her dramatic eyes with very subtle shades on her lips and cheeks: this look is all about eyes, and flashy red lipstick or deep blush would lessen the impact of those gorgeous peepers.

3. Mascara

Were you blessed with long, thick eyelashes? If not, mascara can be your best friend. The trick, however, is to **apply it so that your lashes still look natural**. You don't want to walk around with tarantulas on your eyes!

First, a few practical pointers. Number one, no matter how many times you've seen someone pump the wand into the mascara tube twenty times before applying it, don't do it! This only forces air into the tube and causes your mascara to dry out. Just insert the wand gently, and voilà! The mascara still comes out—and more evenly at that. Number two: remember that mascara can be a breeding ground for bacteria, so don't keep a tube for more than six months, no matter how rarely you use it.

Apply mascara to every lash on your top lashes, giving an extra coat to outer lashes. Have an eyelash comb handy to remove clumps. Always use less mascara on your bottom lashes.

Black mascara gives a really dramatic effect. If you'd like a softer, more natural look, try a **brown or dark brown** mascara. If you're feeling adventurous, try out some of the **color mascaras**, such as cobalt blue or green. Use these sparingly, however, since they have a tendency to be really bright. If you already have lush lashes, or if you are a natural redhead or blonde with lashes to match that you don't want to cover up, try using a **clear mascara**.

♥ **Here's a tip:**

If you have problems with your mascara running, don't apply any at all to the bottom lashes, which are the ones that tend to run. (Another alternative is to use waterproof mascara, but some people don't like it because it is hard to remove.)

Maybelline spokesmodel **Sarah Michelle Gellar** dresses up her pretty green eyes with pale earth-toned shadows and a coat of brown mascara. While black mascara works on just about anyone, blondes and redheads might consider opting for other shades, or even clear mascara, which separates and thickens lashes without adding color, for a more casual look.

4. Eyebrows

Don't overlook your eyebrows! You don't want to take attention away from your beautifully made-up eyes with an unruly set of brows.

Natural is always your best bet, so if you have to tweeze, don't go nuts. If you're unsure about what to do, let a **professional** tweeze or wax your eyebrows, at least for the first time. Not only will she make your brows nice and even, she can help you find the shape that's right for your face. Having your eyebrows done is relatively inexpensive, between $8 and $20 at most salons. When you think about the damage you could end up doing, it's worth the money!

♥ **Here's a tip:**

To keep your newly shaped eyebrows in place, apply a little bit of **gel** to your brows using an eyebrow brush—or try a coat of clear mascara.

Creating the Illusion

None of us has perfectly positioned facial features, and for most of us, that means our eyes are usually too close together, too far apart, or too deep-set. If any of these eye types sounds like you, try one of these makeup tricks.

Close-Set Eyes, like Kellie Martin:

Line the outer corner of your upper and lower eyelids. Apply lighter shades of eye shadow to the inner corner of your eyelid and darker shades to the outer corner.

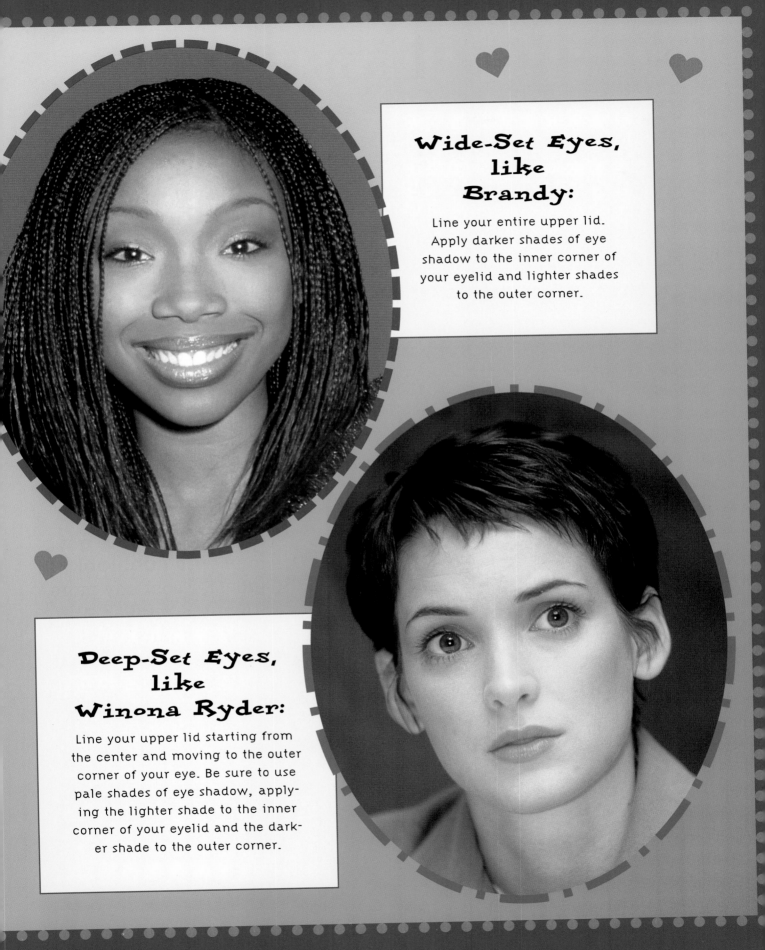

Wide-Set Eyes, like Brandy:

Line your entire upper lid. Apply darker shades of eye shadow to the inner corner of your eyelid and lighter shades to the outer corner.

Deep-Set Eyes, like Winona Ryder:

Line your upper lid starting from the center and moving to the outer corner of your eye. Be sure to use pale shades of eye shadow, applying the lighter shade to the inner corner of your eyelid and the darker shade to the outer corner.

Lips

Lipstick is the finishing touch for the perfectly made-up face.

Next to your eyes, your lips will be the feature that gets the most attention, so you want to make sure they look good!

First and foremost, make sure your lips are **well moisturized**. Whether you wear lipstick or not, there aren't many things less attractive than cracked, peeling lips. Keep a tube of **lip balm** on you at all times. Be sure to get one with **sunblock**; it doesn't cost any more than the regular stuff and not only will it keep your lips soft but it will protect them from dangerous UV rays, which can really damage your lips.

Pucker up: nothing is more kissable than soft, healthy lips. **Salma Hayek** dresses hers up with a liner and lipcolor in pink shades, with a coat of gloss for extra shine.

Before you apply lipstick to those luscious lips of yours, you might want to start out with a **lip liner**. While not a necessity, a properly applied lip liner will give your lips definition and shape, and can keep your lipstick from feathering around the edges. The key word here is "properly." Here's how:

- ♥ Find a shade of lip liner that most closely matches your lipstick.

- ♥ Resist the urge to apply your lip liner all the way to the corner of your lips. The top and bottom lip liner outlines should not meet.

- ♥ Shade over your entire lip with your lip liner. This way, should your lipstick wear off, you won't be left with a nasty-looking lip liner outline.

And finally, the lipstick. **For daytime, stick with more natural-colored lipsticks** or lip glosses—save your more daring shades for the evening. If you're still wearing your braces (and don't feel bad— we've all been there), avoid bright, flashy lipstick colors. Stick with more subdued shades so that attention won't be drawn straight to your lips.

Don't feel like you have to coat every millimeter of your lips with a thick layer of lipstick. If you do this, not only will your lipstick wear off faster, you won't be able to eat anything— or kiss anyone—until it does! Here are a few tips for perfect lips:

- ♥ Apply a thin layer of lipstick, barely covering your lips.

- ♥ Then press your lips together and move them around to spread the lipstick.

- ♥ Finally, blot the excess on a tissue or napkin— and you're ready to face the world!

Britney Spears has been known to take her makeup to extremes on stage, but her everyday look is fairly simple. When she's not in performance mode, she usually opts for a palette of earthy neutrals that complement her brown eyes and tawny skin. Paired with a shiny coat of lip gloss, it's a stunning but casual makeup look.

Body Art

This is an exciting—but risky!—way to give the world a healthy dose of your personal style.

A tattoo on your ankle, your shoulder, your hip—all are ways to express what you love, what you think, what you feel. But remember, more so than a diamond, **a tattoo is forever**. You might really love Evan or Neil or Paul (or butterflies, stars, or hearts for that matter), but there's no need to brand yourself.

And let's not forget the pain!

What's a tattoo? It's ink injected—yes, with a needle—into your skin. The injection goes deep, which is why a tattoo doesn't wash off with your dead skin. And **tattoo removal is painful and very expensive**, requiring many visits over a period of time. Removal also costs a lot of money, and there's no guarantee that even when you're through, there won't still be a faint reminder. And, oh yeah, let's also not forget that your folks will probably kill you for getting one!

Drew Barrymore's rose-encrusted cross tattoo looks great with her retro-style dress and funky patent leather platforms. If you'd like to get the look without the commitment, check out henna tattoos, which look great and last just a few weeks.

True enough, a tattoo is a personal expression, but that doesn't mean you have to do any permanent damage to have one. **Experiment with temporary tattoos.** Available at novelty shops, they're fun, inexpensive, and best of all, totally removable. For special occasions, a custom-made temporary tattoo is the ultimate accessory. Or for something more lasting, try a **henna version**. Henna tattoos have been around for thousands of years, they're painless, and they wash off in one to three weeks. Henna tattoos have become a hot fashion accessory.

Who needs jewelry when you can have the perfect, dazzling accessory land right on your shoulders? **Kirsten Dunst** sported a hand-painted dragonfly across her back at the *Drop Dead Gorgeous* premiere.

What do these tattoos say about their wearers?

Manicures and Pedicures

Believe it or not,
our finger- and toenails affect our overall style package.

Like a pretty bow that finishes off a nicely wrapped present, our nails can add *that perfect finishing touch of style and color.*

And unlike your hair and makeup, which you only see when you look in a mirror, you can enjoy your own nails all day long.

> A French manicure is a classic nail treatment in which the tips of the nails are painted white, followed by a coat of clear or almost-clear polish over the whole nail. It's a clean, natural look that works best on shorter nails.

It doesn't take much time to keep up with your finger-nails. If you generally **keep your hands clean**, you're practically there. If you like gardening, **wear gloves**!

Are you a nail biter?

You'd better cut that out soon. Not only does this habit make your fingers look stubby, but it makes you look sloppy and insecure. Losing the habit is hard, but it can be done. Yours truly was a nail biter for a long time. Here's a trick that helped me: Every time you get the urge to gnaw at your nails, think of how bad it makes your nails look—and how foolish you look with your fingers in your mouth. You'll be reformed in no time! Now don't be alarmed when your nails grow in a little bumpy. That will grow out in a few weeks and then you'll be set to give your fingernails the attention they deserve.

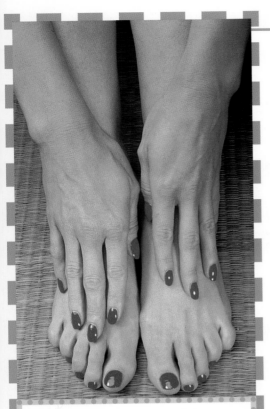

Taking the time out to take care of your fingers and toes can really make a difference. With or without polish, neat, manicured nails tell people that you're secure and confident.

- ♥ Start by filing those rough edges with an emery board. A round shape is pretty, but a square tip is stronger.

- ♥ Then soak your fingertips in some warm water for a few minutes to soften up your cuticles.

- ♥ Massage your nailbeds with a bit of cuticle cream before gently pushing your cuticles back toward the base of your nail with the slanted edge of a wooden orange stick.

- ♥ Don't cut your cuticles (and don't let your manicurist do it, either); trimmed cuticles may look great on the day of your manicure, but they grow back rough and ragged, and bring on those nasty (and painful) hangnails.

- ♥ Polish is a nice touch, but well-tended hands and feet can go without for a natural look; use a buffer to give them a soft shine.

- ♥ If you do decide to go *au naturel*, you may opt to gloss those nails over with a clear polish to strengthen and protect them.

Don't think you have to be completely traditional with how you decorate your finger- and toenails. **Try out new designs.** Why not dress up one nail with a small jewel to be elegant or a fun sticker if you're feeling playful? And as for your toes—well, that's where you can have the most fun! **Wild colors** that seem too weird or unflattering for your fingers are perfect for your toes.

What good are open-toed shoes if you don't have a proper pedicure? Give your feet extra attention in the summertime to keep them looking and feeling great.

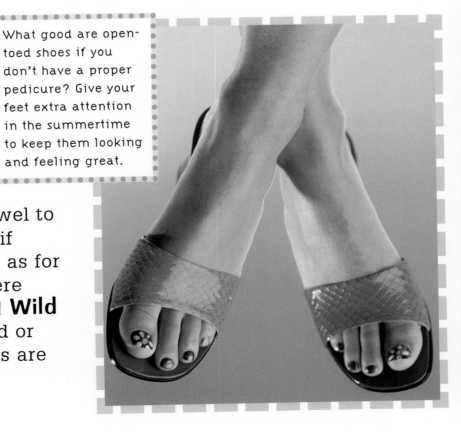

Chapter  2

Taming the 'Do

What do you do with your 'do?

It's a question we all face in the morning. **Your hair is one of the most important components of your style package.** How you wear it says a lot about you, your attitude, your outlook, your sense of style.

Rebecca Romjin-Stamos keeps it simple but stunning for a Hollywood premiere. Her blonde, shoulder-length locks are trimmed in long layers that frame her face, and kept in control with a smoothing glaze. Cut and texture are important here: Rebecca's hair is long enough to tuck behind her ears, with a few not-so wispy chunks falling forward to keep it casual but glamorous.

How important is hair? Just think of all the celebs who are best known for their hair: Lil' Kim, Jennifer Aniston, Keri Russell—even Sinead O'Connor for her lack of hair!

When our hair looks good, it's our best friend. When we have a **good hair day**, we feel confident, secure, upbeat. But when it frizzes, flops, flies away, knots, or is just plain unruly, it can totally ruin our mood. And let's face it, nothing ruins a style more than bad hair. Whether it's just misbehaving or that the cut or color you've chosen just doesn't work for you, **bad hair can be a fashion disaster.**

Those eyes, that smile—why would **Brandy** hide it all behind a distracting head of hair? Her classic braids are simple and versatile: worn up off of her face, they highlight her beautiful cheekbones and eyes.

So how do you do your 'do?

This chapter will give you examples of how hair defines a style, from long hair to short to bald; from natural to vibrant **colors**; from **updos** to dreads to **weaves** and extensions.

Lisa
Ling's got an enviable head of luscious long hair, but even she gets bored with letting it just fall around her face all day. Here, she pulls her hair back in sections, and twists it into a crown of tiny swirls. Fastened with hairpins, it's a simple and casual way to keep a long mane out of your face with style.

Changing your look doesn't require a ton of money or a personal stylist. Some styling gel and rollers can get you the loose curls **Christina Aguilera** sports here—a far cry from her usual pin-straight locks.

If the Hair Fits...

Here's the scenario: Jenna, who sits in front of you in biology, just came back to school Monday morning with a new haircut. She looked so fabulous that you decided to try it out for yourself. And even though you described the look perfectly to your hairdresser (in fact, you even snapped a photo of Jenna when she wasn't looking!), the style just didn't cut it on you. In fact, you came back to school the following Monday looking like a stomped mushroom. No chance anyone was going to accuse you of being a copycat. Everyone gave Jenna admiring looks—but they greeted you with pity and even laughter. So what went wrong?

It's simple, really. The reason a particular hairstyle looks really good on one person and like Medusa's snakes on another has to do with more factors than just your hair itself. In addition to the **amount**, **thickness,** and **texture** of your hair, which affect the way your hair holds a particular style, **the shape of your face** and your features, the size of your head, and even your height all factor in to **what hairstyle will look best on you**. Can you imagine Jennifer Lopez with a crew cut? Or Halle Berry with tresses down to her knees? Of course not! If you take the time to learn about yourself and talk your options over with your hair stylist before he or she picks up the scissors, you'll be much happier after the chop.

Choosing a Hairstyle That Suits You

Take a good look at your head in the mirror.

Feel it with your hands. Nobody has a perfectly smooth, round head, so don't worry about the bumps! Take note of where your head is flat and where it curves and choose a style accordingly. For example, if your head is kind of flat in the back, choose a style to "round off" your head. In *In Style*, stylist Frederic Fekkai recommends a look in which your hair falls longer at the crown, with razor-cut layers to round off the 'do.

Determine your face shape.

Is it oval, square, round, pear-shaped, or heart-shaped? Each of these demands a different solution. For example, if you have a heart-shaped face, a chin-length look may be just what the stylist ordered to create a sense of width around your chin. For a pear-shaped face, you'll want to pull attention away from your cheeks. This is easily accomplished with classic layered looks.

What kind of build do you have?

Fekkai also recommends that you work with your body type. For example, if you are petite in stature, you should consider close-cropped styles that don't add jarring height. A fuller style generally works better with a larger build.

What's your

Cameron Diaz: Round

Cameron's typical layered bob is perfect for her round head. It lifts and narrows her face, giving it a more oval appearance.

Christina Aguilera: Heart-Shaped

While Christina goes through a bevy of styles—like most of our style icons—there's no question what looks best on her: long, full, and bouncy. This cut is perfect for drawing attention away from the pointy chin that goes along with having a heart-shaped head.

head shape?

Jada Pinkett Smith: Oval

With her oval face, Jada Pinkett Smith could wear just about any hair style. But at just under five feet tall, Jada might look lost with a mane of long, flowing locks. The short, perky styles she tends to favor complement her diminutive stature and finely drawn features.

Keri Russell: Square

Keri has great hair that she knows how to wear with her square face. Now short, it maintains a round and soft effect, with height at the crown, which helps to round off the edges of a square face.

Getting It Straight

Straight hair is chic and sexy. It's sleek and elegant and extremely versatile. Some people are born with straight hair, while others really have to work at it. Take *Friends* cast member Jennifer Aniston. Her hair is totally straight and fell perfectly down her back, right? Guess again. Jennifer actually has wavy hair, which had to be blown out for hours every time she hit the set!

Jennifer Aniston's wavy hair got the straightening treatment every time she hit the set on *Friends*. While you might love the look, Jennifer will be the first one to admit that all that damaging heat took its toll on her hair—that's why she cut it all off!

Supermodel Irina's naturally straight hair benefits from long layers and shaggy bangs, both of which add body and bounce, and prevent the length from weighing her hair down.

One of the biggest problems the straight of hair face is **flyaways**. No problem—you can put those unruly hairs in their place by matting them down with a bit of gel, or if you're in a bind, a teensy bit of hand lotion. (Rub a dab of lotion thoroughly into your hands, then quickly run your fingers through your hair. Don't use too much lotion, though, or your hair will look greasy rather than just slick.)

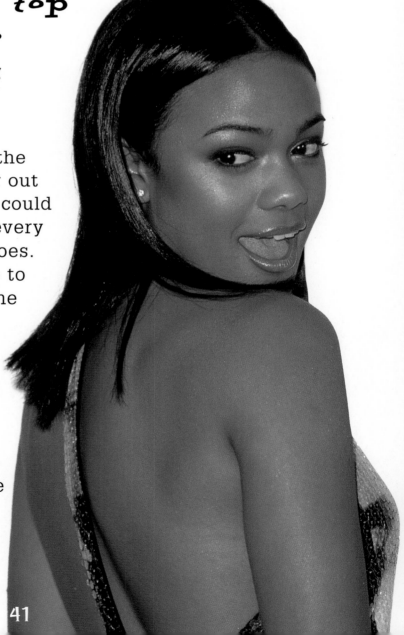

Fresh Prince co-star turned star in her own right **Tatiyana Ali** gets the sleek, straight treatment on her long locks. Lots of conditioner and an anti-humectant pomade add shine while protecting her hair from heat and chemicals.

Are you a curly top who pines for straight locks like Jennifer?

Well, you don't have to adopt the old method of spreading your hair out on an ironing board to get it. You could work a **blow dryer** on that hair every day, much like Jennifer's stylist does. If that's what you choose, be sure to use a **good conditioner** since the heat of the dryer can really damage your hair. (See page 58 for tips on improving your hair.) Another method you could try is to have your hair **chemically straightened** at the hair salon. But keep in mind that this is very damaging to your hair, and can be expensive to boot. If you don't have naturally straight hair, it's probably better to learn to work with your natural waves.

Straight or curly, long or short, there's no reason for you to be stuck with the same hair every day. A few hair pins, rubber bands, or **groovy barrettes** and you can take your hair in **entirely new directions**—just for today. Try pulling your hair off your face with a regular headband—use a thick leather or suede one for a thick mane of hair, or a whisper thin wire or lingerie strap one if you have fine hair. Or pull that hair back off your face with an **entire army** of bobby pins, braids, or tiny hair clips.

Want your long hair off your shoulders as well as your face? Pull it back into a tight ponytail, and instead of fastening it with a rubber band, give that ponytail a little twist and secure it to the back of your head with a barrette or clip. Let the top wisp down like a water fountain and you've got a simple but killer updo!

When it comes to fastening your long hair in a killer updo, it pays to think outside the box. Pulled straight back and twisted upwards, **Kirsten Dunst**'s straight blonde locks fan out behind her head like the spray of a water fountain. The whole 'do is held in place by a pair of chopsticks.

Buns aren't just for bal-lerinas anymore. Sculpt your hair into forms nature never intended with some styling gel, and maybe a bit of help in the form of a roller or a bit of wire, as **Irina** has done here. Paired with her straight-as-a-pin bangs, this torpedo-shaped bun is almost architectural.

Even vampire slayers like to get dolled up once in a while, and what could be more sophisticat-ed than a pile of twirly curls cas-cading down around your head? *Buffy*'s **Alyson Hannigan** and **Sarah Michelle Gellar** wore romantic updos to the MTV Music Awards.

Curly Tops

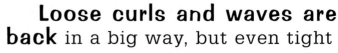

Loose curls and waves are **back** in a big way, but even tight natural curls are totally hot these days. Curly locks create a **full and romantic** look. A long curly mane is **sexy and stunning**—worn down, it's an instant attention grabber. Julia Roberts, Andie MacDowell, and Keri Russell are all known for their curly locks as well as for their acting accomplishments.

Long curly ringlets like **Rebecca Gayheart**'s are stunning, but can be hard to manage—when the humidity goes up, those curls can get frizzy or even down right bushy. To tame that mane, try an anti-humectant pomade, and try to let your hair dry naturally. When there's no time to wait, use a diffuser with your blowdryer to avoid flattening out your curls.

Do you already have a head full of curls, or do you want to capture the look?

If you're a straighty wanting to go curly, you've got **plenty of options**, ranging from temporary experiments to hitting the salon for a full-blown permanent. **But if you're thinking permanent, think again:** like straightening, perms are very hard on your hair. And many salons won't give perms to girls (or boys) under sixteen because **the chemicals they use are so toxic**, and because perms are unlikely to hold well on such young hair.

Curls Without Commitment

But you don't need to get a permanent to have curls once in a while. Want to try out being curly gradually, or just wear a glamorous mane for one special event? **Temporary curls** have been a major fashion trend lately among the Hollywood elite. You can get the look by investing in some inexpensive **hair rollers**. For a really loose curl, wrap dry hair around large rollers. For really tight curls, your best bet is to wrap wet hair around tiny rollers.

Another way to generate waves is to put several **braids** in each section of your hair before you go to sleep. More braids equals more volume—and wet means tighter waves than dry. But be patient: those tight wet locks will take a long time to dry! If you want the waves without the wait, check out **hot rollers** or **curling irons**. Each comes in a variety of sizes, and can create lots of different, great looks in hardly any time at all.

❀ **The main drawback of curly or wavy hair is frizz!**

It's the biggest complaint of all curly tops and it's what makes them dread the summer and humidity the most. But never fear—there are plenty of products out there to help you **tame that mane**, from pomades to mousses. Experiment to see which of these suits your hair best.

Hair today, gone tomorrow: **Halle Berry** usually sports a sophisticated short 'do, but has been known to indulge in a mane of long curls occasionally, via wigs and extensions.

Everyday Hair

It's easy for curly hair to become big and busy without proper care. **Kate Hudson**'s cascade of waves is kept manageable with a long, loose cut. Best of all, it looks best when it dries naturally—no blow drying!

Lauryn Hill's trademark braids always look great, and once they're in, require precious little maintenance. They're the perfect complement to Lauryn's unique brand of no-nonsense glamour.

Okay, so not everybody has a stylist waiting every morning to transform them into perfectly coiffed divas. But just because you don't have the time or money to get your curls blown out, your long hair ironed flat, or extensions woven in doesn't mean that you can't look great. Lots of celebs who could go for more elaborate looks often opt for simple, comfortable hair that looks awesome without being a ton of work. Take a look at some of these options.

Sandra Bullock usually wears her hair straight and simple. Whatever length she chooses, her style often says that she's interested in more than just her hair, and that makes her natural beauty really shine.

Michelle Kwan needs a style that can take a few turns without looking like she's been through the spin cycle—even when she has! From the long (that is, bun-friendly) look of her early teens to the short, sassy style she moved into in the late nineties to her current mid-length shag, she's gone from one low-maintenance look to another without ever looking anything less than perfect.

Liv Tyler shocked everyone when she chopped her endless locks for a pixie cut just a few inches long, but it just goes to show how far a good face can take you! And Liv's not alone. Many babes have traded in their long locks for short hair at one time or another (think of Keri Russell, or Winona Ryder), and for good reason.

Why Go Short?

There are many benefits in having short hair. **Easy daily maintenance** is pretty high on the list—short hair requires less time to wash, rinse, and style, all of which are especially important for active girls (plus, it's nice to avoid getting slapped with your own ponytail at soccer practice). With the right short haircut, getting ready in the morning could mean nothing more than running your fingers through your hair. And **short hair flatters a pretty face**, highlighting cheekbones and giving more attention to small features.

Liv Tyler's thick, long locks were something of a trademark, so when she cut them off for this cropped pixie 'do, fashion-watchers were shocked, to say the least. But Liv knew that she could put more of a focus on her pretty face—not to mention her acting skills—if she got that hair out of the way.

Those who wear short hair best—like **Halle Berry**—know to play up their features with strong color on their eyes and lips, and simple but striking jewelry on their ears and around their necks.

A perfect face doesn't need much at all in the way of embellishment—just take a look **Bai Ling** with a quarter-inch crop that makes the most of her stunning features. And it's fun to touch, too.

With the right cut, products, and accessories, short hair can go sporty or slick, modern or retro.

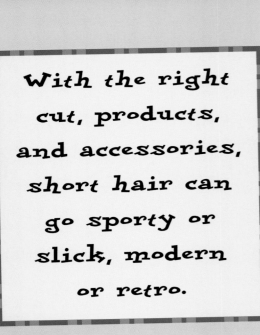

Classic Long Locks

Not many attributes of style are sexier than a long and luscious head of hair. Portia de Rossi, Jessica Simpson, Daisy Fuentes, Courteney Cox Arquette, Tyra Banks—these gals have hair to spare and they really know how to wear it.

Long-haired beauties have so many options.

If your hair is long, you can wear it **loose and free-flowing**, cascading down your shoulders and blowing in the breeze. And what about special occasions and all the **updos** you can do? The options are limitless: buns, twists, braids, knots—it's a stylist's dream.

But special occasions aside, a long head of hair can be an everyday nightmare. The main drawback of really long hair is the **high maintenance**. It takes forever to wash. You have to be meticulous to get all the shampoo out of every strand. Then you end up spending half your life blow-drying it and the other half brushing it! And your parents know all too well the havoc it wreaks on the drains in your shower and sink!

Long hair is not for everyone—and for more reasons than the above. **Sometimes it just doesn't look right on a person**.

Who wouldn't want a stream of honey blonde tresses like **Daisy Fuentes**'? Cascading down around her shoulders, it's a dream—but washing, drying, and styling a head of hair like Daisy's can be a nightmare.

Remember Meg Ryan in *Sleepless in Seattle*? Okay, she looked good. She always looks good. But with long hair, she did not look half as good as she does in *You've Got Mail*. That shorter shag is the style that really suits her.

Remember Marcia Brady? Her smooth, straight locks owed more to genetics than to style. As much as you might want this look, remember that you'll look ten times better with a style your hair can actually hold.

Long, cool, and elegant, **Bai Ling**'s long hair is kept manageable yet sophisticated with a simple ponytail and brow-length bangs. It's a timeless look that doesn't take too much time.

Hair Today, Gone Tomorrow

With no bangs or hair jewelry, **Aaliyah**'s long tresses accentuate her beautiful features without overpowering them.

Of course, there are many alternatives to actually growing your hair long. How does Jennifer Aniston manage to have shoulder-length hair in January and waist-length hair in June? How can Britney and Christina have really long hair for some shows and their regular shoulder-length or shorter hair for others? Yep, you guessed it: hair **extensions**. The best part about these is that **they also let you play with color and texture**. Do you have really thin hair? Try extensions in a thicker texture and see how the other half lives. And if you're really daring, why not **try out a wig**—or seven—like the Queen Bee!

Head Gear

Tired of the same old thing? Well, your hair doesn't have to be all hair—a few simple accessories can **dress up your hair**, giving you a whole new look without changing the cut or color that you already know and love. Take a trip to the department store, the drugstore—even the garden—and add a little something to that 'do.

Some off-the-wall makeup and a pair of funky clips make supermodel **Irina's** very simple haircut look simply outrageous, proving that taking a walk on the wild side doesn't necessarily mean cutting, dying, or frying your hair!

A crown of little butterflies, and **Mandy Moore** is ready to take off. This is a fun little 'do that anyone can do: just grab your hair in sections, twist each section back, and clip it in place.

Earth-child **Drew Barrymore** really shone at the 1998 Academy Awards, and with nary a sparkle in sight. A few daisies strewn about her short wavy locks was all she needed to make a delightful fashion statement.

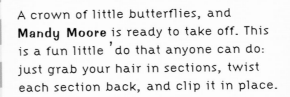

Choosing a Hair Color

How many of us wish that nature had provided us with shiny, healthy, richly colored **manes of gold, red, chestnut, ebony**? Sure, a few of you may have been blessed by nature, but as for the rest of us, well, we need to be more ingenious.

Are you a natural redhead or blonde? Maybe you were at one time, but then puberty took its toll on your locks and left you mousy brown. That's right—while your body's busy going through all those other changes, don't be surprised if the color of your hair is affected, too. **But you can mess with Mother Nature.**

Eve traded in her trademark almost-bald bleach job for a slightly longer and more colorful crop that looks just as stunning. Without straying too far from what she was really comfortable with, she's created a whole new look.

One alternative is the all-or-nothing approach,

where you buy a bottle of your favorite shade, pour it over your head (following the directions on the box, natch)—and presto! Instant change. These products are available in drug stores, and range from semi-permanent to permanent.

Keep in mind that the more permanent they are, the more likely they are to damage your hair or irritate your scalp. Also, if you don't like the shade, you'll be stuck with it for a while.

Of course, you might opt for a more gradual change, by adding highlights.

Many products are available for adding these color streaks to your hair, but if you're not sure about your abilities in this department, your best bet is to enlist an experienced pal—an older sister, your mom, or even better, **invest in the services of a professional**. Sure, you might have to drop more than a few nights' baby-sitting proceeds, but not looking like a mutant zebra will be worth the investment!

If you go for a full-color makeover, be sure to touch it up every four weeks or so. If you highlight, you can go as long as three months between touchups.

Another alternative is to try wash-out color treatments,

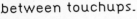

which generally last about from four to six weeks. If you're not really sure you want to be a redhead, it's better to walk around with a carrot top for a couple of weeks than to wait until a more permanent red hair dye completely grows out. And if you color over that look, you can't be sure you're going to get your natural color back.

Christina Aguilera manages to change her 'do almost daily with the help of extensions. They add not only length and texture, but also color, as with the black-and-red ones she's wearing here.

Whatever you decide to do with your hair, be sure to **discuss it with your parents first**—there's no sense in changing your hair if it will get you grounded.

If you only want a **particular look** for a **special occasion**, why not follow Lil' Kim's lead and **try out a wig or two**? One second you're a blonde, and the next second, a redhead. It's a painless alternative—for you and your hair!

They don't call her **Pink** for nothing. With a head of spiky candy-colored locks, she's sure to get a lot of attention. But think twice before you try this at home!

What's that on Left Eye's head? TLC's **Lisa Lopez** has a little fun with a long, burgundy wig. Short bangs and a pair of thick ropy braids work well with her sporty but still glamorous look.

You probably won't want to change your hair color as often as your fave celeb does. After all, they have a staff of professionals tending to their every need to make sure their hair doesn't get damaged, or to fix it up if it does.

Besides, if you were to change your hair color as often as Dennis Rodman, your friends just might not recognize you from one week to the next.

No Doubt front woman **Gwen Stefani** changes her hair color as often as the mood strikes her, going from her natural dark blond to platinum blonde to just about any color in your Crayola eight pack.

Tips

for Stronger, Healthier Hair

Do you have more bad hair days than good?

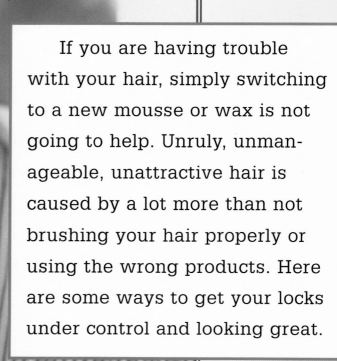

If you are having trouble with your hair, simply switching to a new mousse or wax is not going to help. Unruly, unmanageable, unattractive hair is caused by a lot more than not brushing your hair properly or using the wrong products. Here are some ways to get your locks under control and looking great.

Have a Trim.

Even if you're trying to grow your hair out, you should get the ends trimmed every four to six weeks. This will get rid of dead, split ends—and will even help your hair grow faster!

Get a Lube Job.

How many **hot oil treatments** have you had in the past six months? What about in the past year? These help make your hair shiny and manageable. A few **products** are available in your local drug store, but you can also use **olive oil**—right from the pantry. For a really deep treatment, wrap your oiled mane up in a **hot towel** just pulled from the dryer.

Treat Your Hair.

If hot oil isn't your thing, show your hair how much you love and appreciate it by giving it a thorough **conditioning treatment** at least once a month.

Detox.

As much as you love your favorite hair products, they will build up in your hair over time and weigh it down. You need to **vary your routine** every few months or so. Before you change shampoos, take a week to **detoxify** your hair with a shampoo specially designed to remove buildup from your hair. Check out the new **chelation** shampoos—but don't use these more than once a month or you may really damage your hair. Or try a home remedy for product buildup: Rinse with a cup of **apple cider vinegar**.

Rinse with Cold Water.

This little trick will really make your hair shine.

Take Care of Yourself.

If you don't **eat properly, get enough sleep,** and **drink enough water,** or if you stress out too much, your hair will be affected. It might become limp, flyaway, or just an all-around disaster!

Chapter 3
Dress
to
Impress

Brandy styles hard in a fuschia sequined half-tank—the perfect complement to snug-fitting, cuffed jeans. A pair of chunky Candies comfortably add a few inches to the dishy diva's height, while giving her a chance to show off a perfect pedicure.

What bigger statement of style is there than the clothes we wear?

What we wear tells the people around us who we are.

While the beauty of clothes means **you can change your style like you change your underwear**, eventually you'll hit on just the style that makes you look good—and **feel good**. After all, if you feel self-conscious and awkward in a halter top, chances are you're not going to be perceived as a high school sex goddess—you'll more likely appear like a small child playing dress up. Can you say "fashion emergency"?

The way clothes work on us is determined by a number of factors, including our **height**, **build**, **hair length**, and most importantly, our **personalities**. So remember, what works for Britney Spears works for Britney Spears—but might not work for the Olsen twins. And can you imagine Natalie Portman in a fuchsia sequined halter top and teal vinyl pants? Absolutley not, but for Christina Aguilera, what could be more fitting?

Read on for **great tips** from your favorite celebrities on clothes for work and play, formal wear, and workout wear. In the last chapter, you'll see how to tie your look together with a few cleverly chosen **accessories**!

Natalie Portman's buttoned-up denim jacket, simple shoulder bag, and demurely pulled back hair are proof positive that simplicity is sometimes the best ticket to style.

Everyday Style
Clothes for School, Work, and Play

How many mornings have you woken up late for school and reeled back in horror in front of your closet when you realized **you had nothing to wear**? Your closet might be stuffed to the rafters and your dresser drawers spilling over with clothes—and yet there's still that sense of dread. And it doesn't just happen to us before school. We have the same horrors for work and play. **How can you make getting dressed in the morning a little easier?**

The biggest favor you can do for yourself when you head out on your next shopping spree is to not let yourself get bogged down in fads.

Part of the reason it seems like you have nothing to wear is that you get sick of your trendy clothes—or they go out of style by the first time you wash them! While it's fun to have a few pieces in your wardrobe that are funky and "today," be sure to have plenty of **classics** as well.

Jessica Simpson relaxes on the beach in casual blue denim—is she perhaps on a date with her beloved Nick Lachey? The red bandanna—a style innovation brought into the fashion mainstream by Kelly of Survivor—is a great casual way to hold back her long blonde tresses.

A classic is a piece of clothing that never goes out of style.

A simple black dress. Basic blue jeans. A black turtleneck. A white T-shirt.

Of course, you don't want to skimp on the **trends** altogether. After all, these are what make your wardrobe fun and up to date. **How can you update a classic and give it a more trendy look? Try accessories.** A colorful **scarf**. A wicked pair of **earrings**. The perfect, cutting-edge **shoes**. You'll learn more about these in the chapter on accessories.

Also, keep in mind that whether you're going to school or to work or just hanging out with your friends, you don't want to look like you've just shown up to paint the garage. **Grunge is way out, girlfriend!** Courtney Love learned that lesson and traded in her tattered baby doll dresses and disheveled hair for a glam new look.

Jennifer Lopez has a knack for taking a classic look and reinterpreting it for an up-to-the-minute edgy effect. Her sparkling three-quarter sleeve, bateau-necked sweater and street-length leather skirt are timeless shapes updated in trendy new textures.

Today, being in style is all about looking good.

It's about creating a style that's all your own, and wearing it with pride, whether that means decking out like a diva or wrapping yourself in your fave Banana Republic sweater.

Formal

A formal occasion is your chance to really shine. Whether it's for a **prom**, a cousin's wedding—or the Grammy Awards if you happen to be a pop star—how you **glam up** says a lot about **who you are** and your personal sense of style.

There are lots of ways to go **glam**. The **traditional gown** is an eternal favorite. Few things are more romantic than a long, flowing gown. Add sequins or beads—ooh-la-la! Of course, gowns are worn for only the most formal occasions. There are other times when a **cocktail dress** really fits the bill. These generally hit at or above the knee, so you can have some fun showing off a little leg! And ever since Sharon Stone wore a Gap T-shirt and pair of pants to the Academy Awards a few years back, **pants** for formal occasions have been way in vogue—but the dress-down thing is still a bit tough to pull off at formal events! Of course, a well-chosen pant suit can do the job of even the sexiest dress.

The most important objective is to wear something that suits you, and that makes you feel gorgeous and totally comfortable at the same time.

Just because a particular color or style catches your fancy doesn't mean that should be your dream dress. When you're searching for that perfect ensemble, **try on** as many as your mom or your friends—or whomever you're shopping with—can possibly stand. There's one thing about the perfect formal dress—you'll just know it's the one as soon as you put it on!

Bring It On! **Kirsten Dunst** dazzled spectators at the Sixth Annual Screen Actor's Guild Awards in this olive green satin sheath.

Natalie Portman was a classic beauty in an off-the-shoulder number in basic black at the 2000 Golden Globes.

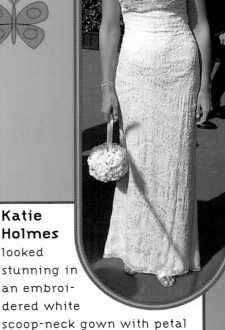

Katie Holmes looked stunning in an embroidered white scoop-neck gown with petal sleeves. A flowered bag was the perfect finishing touch.

The combo of shimmering skirt and sequined top in bright tangerine helped **Sarah Michelle Gellar** slay onlookers at *Saturday Night Live*'s Twenty-fifth Anniversary celebration.

What to Wear?!
What to Wear?!

Are you stuck trying to find the **right dress** for a **special occasion**? Don't worry, girlfriend. Everyone hits a roadblock like that—and the more special the occasion, the harder it is to find the right thing to wear. Here's a breakdown of things to pay attention to in **formal wear**. If you don't have a personal stylist—um, like most of us—use this as a guide to decide what type of dress will work best for you.

Lengths

The length of your dress is really a **personal decision**, but here are **some guidelines** for various occasions to wear one length rather than another.

A floor-length gown just touches the floor. It is reserved for the most formal occasion, such as in this example where **Tia and Tamara Mowry** wore floor-length numbers to the Soul Train Awards.

Ankle-length gowns

stop at the ankle—so your shoes really matter! Like the floor-length gown, this type of dress is also meant for special occasions. Here, **Christina Aguilera** wears an ankle-length gown to the *Essence* Awards 2000.

A tea-length dress,

one that stops at mid-calf, is appropriate for less formal occasions—for a seasonal dance versus a prom. While **Anna Paquin** wore a floor-length gown to the Academy Awards, a tea-length skirt was more appropriate for a movie premiere.

Street-length dresses and minis

are worn to all kinds of less-formal events, from dance parties to movie premieres. The street length falls to the knee, as worn by **Daisy Fuentes**, while the mini generally ends one to two inches above the knee.

The micro-mini

is for the most adventurous dressers. Usually stopping more than two inches above the knee, the micro-mini makes a fun statement and shows off great legs. **Jennifer Lopez** is a classic micro-mini wearer.

Sleeves

Another consideration is what type of sleeve suits you best. Is it a warm-weather event, or will you be cold in a sleeveless number? This section will show you **a few of the sleeve types** available.

Cap sleeves

are great if you've been working out your arms and want to show them off. These tiny sleeves just barely cover the top of **Michelle Kwan**'s shoulders.

Fitted sleeves

go the distance, from shoulder to wrist, and hug the arm. **Monica** wears them here. They work best in wintertime when you want that extra coverage. A variation of the fitted sleeve is the pointed sleeve, in which the sleeve ends in a point over the wrist.

Petal sleeves

look just as you'd imagine. They are generally short, and loop over the arms. **Reese Witherspoon** wears them here.

Dropped sleeves

are very sophisticated. They can either be short or long, but either way, they must start below the top of the shoulders. **Liv Tyler** wears them here.

Sleeveless

are cut like tank tops or utilize straps with no sleeve at all, and make the most of buff arms and shoulders. They are perfect in the summer, but can be warmed up with long gloves for the most formal events. **Eve** wears them here.

A neckline can determine how sexy a dress is, but it also can be employed to **show off certain features** such as **a long and graceful neck** or to **flatter the shoulders**. Here are some examples.

Necklines

A round neckline (worn by **Tia**) plunges to just above the bust, while **a square neckline** (as seen on **Tamara**—or is that Tia??) dips slightly but crosses from one shoulder to the other in a straight line.

A jewel neckline sits like a necklace, hence the name. Also known as a portrait neckline, it creates a beautiful frame for the face and accentuates a long neck, like **Monica's**.

A sweetheart neckline, as worn here by **Drew Barrymore**, is shaped like a heart and accentuates the bust.

A provocative effect for a provocative babe. **Salma Hayek** shows off what **a halter neckline**, one that wraps around the neck and plunges down to the bustline, does for the wearer. How could Edward Norton resist her?

Neve Campbell shows off **a Sabrina neckline**, a perfect neckline for smaller busted babes. The neckline runs straight from one shoulder to the other. It is also known as a bateau, or boat, neckline.

Workout Chic

Working out is the biggest secret to feeling and looking good, and you'll be more motivated to do it if you have the proper duds for the gym.

The most important concern for choosing workout clothes is **comfort**. Can you move around freely? Are you worried about "bunching up"? Will anything be falling off from being too loose? The best rule is to **wear clothes you don't notice you're wearing**—clothes that won't distract you from your main concern—working that bod!

Monica hits the gym in simple style in a Nike running suit and sports bra combo. When it comes to workout gear, comfort should always come first: choose a bra and shoes that provide good support, and clothes that allow you to stretch and flex with ease.

72

Of course, being comfortable doesn't mean you can't be comfortable in style.

There are lots of great-looking options for every exercise and every sport, from cross-training to cycling to yoga.

What are some essentials of the workout wardrobe?

Number one is definitely a sports bra. Whether you're a double A or triple D, there's nothing more annoying—or uncomfortable—than that extra "bounce" when you're working the Stairmaster or jumping around in your aerobics class.

Other essentials include T-shirts that are just your size—anything tighter will make you feel constricted, anything looser and you'll be distracted by having it fall off your shoulders.

Depending on the weather, shorts or sweats will do for your bottom half.

Chapter 4

Accessorize, Accessorize!

The accessories you choose are the finishing touches to a great style.

Jennifer Love Hewitt has accessorizing down to a style science. Her casual outfit of blue-sleeved white jersey and cords is perfectly accented by a blue chenille scarf and adorable blue-gray chenille hat.

A properly selected **scarf** can make an old and ordinary shirt seem exciting and brand new. A **hat** can be the *pièce de résistance* of a great look. The right **earrings** can flash up a basic black dress. And don't forget about **shoes**: they're the key to keeping any look fresh and up to date.

The most important thing to remember about accessories is that they should be chosen to complement an outfit—not overwhelm it!

Wearing too many extras will make your look cluttered, and depending on what you select, you could end up looking like a bag lady who wears everything she owns at all times. **A few key pieces** can be combined in different ways to **create a variety of hot looks**.

This last chapter will give you examples of the accessories many of your favorite celebrities have chosen to complement their styles and will give you advice on what to wear with what.

Jewelry

Nothing can take you to style extremes like jewelry.

Picture a simple, ordinary, black dress—a staple of any smart wardrobe. Add long, shiny **earrings** and you're ready for a party. A **string of pearls**, and you're off to the opera. A simple **silver choker**, and you're all business. Add more playful jewelry and you've changed the look from dressy to semi-casual.

Jennifer Love Hewitt wears an African bead collar with a subtle diamond heart necklace. A sparkling cuff adds some shine to the earthy look.

Lisa Ling wears jewelry like she wears clothes—at least literally in this ensemble where the dress wraps around the neck like a necklace and is held up with a decorative pin.

Eve always makes a statement—and when it comes to accessories, look out girlfriend! Here, she sports sparkling earrings and groovy glasses. Big earrings and glasses don't always work together—too much ornamentation—but Eve pulls them together beautifully!

There are no hard and fast rules with earrings, but generally, save the long dangling ones for shorter haircuts or days when you wear your hair up. Why? Because if you have long hair and you're wearing it down, you already have an exquisite frame for your face. When you add long earrings into that equation, you run the risk of looking too "busy"—not to mention how annoying it is to get long, dangling, complicated earrings untangled from your hair every three minutes.

Lauryn Hill needs little further adornment—the embroidery on her Mandarin shirt acts as jewelry in and of itself. Silver hoop earrings accented with bright white enamel stand up to her thick, dark braids, completing the perfect look.

Michelle Kwan doesn't go anywhere without her trademark dragon pendant.

The latest trend in necklaces is basically not to wear them at all, but if you do, wear them like they aren't even there—like you somehow have a pendant stuck to the middle of your neck. This means a light, simple, **whisper of a chain** (or even a length of clear fishing line) that really lets the pendant or charm stand out.

And be sure to **keep an eye on the magazines** for inspiration—nothing changes faster than the latest thing celebs are wearing on their necks!

Britney Spears is a devout Christian, and you can usually catch her wearing some symbol of her faith. Here, a tiny silver cross adorns her neck.

Beyonce of Destiny's Child styles hard in big hoop earrings, silver watch, and the perfect finishing touch to well-toned abs—a navel ring.

More fun than what girl-friends are wearing on their wrists today are what they're wearing on their middles: **belly chains**! These are great fun to wear with a half shirt and hip huggers and are big favorites of stars like Britney Spears, Christina Aguilera, and Jennifer Lopez. With so many styles to choose from, you can have one for every occasion!

MTV personality **Ananda Lewis** sparkled in a simple belly chain for the 2000 *Essence* Awards.

Shoes

Don't let anyone ever tell you differently: **an outfit is only as cute, or sexy, or hip as the shoes that finish it off**.

But shoes are more than just a finishing touch. They can set the stage for your whole outfit.

Having trouble deciding what to wear to school today? **Start with picking out the shoes you want to wear and the outfit will create itself**. If there's one time-less rule of fashion, it's this: you can never have too many pairs of shoes.

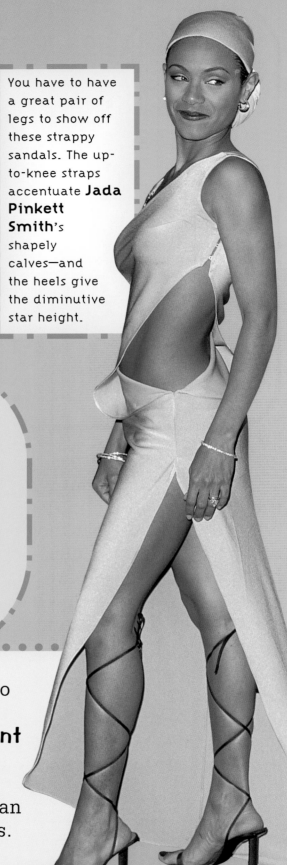

You have to have a great pair of legs to show off these strappy sandals. The up-to-knee straps accentuate **Jada Pinkett Smith**'s shapely calves—and the heels give the diminutive star height.

The first and most important rule of shoe shopping: buy the shoes you **love.**

Shoes can get expensive, so **don't waste your money on shoes that you're not absolutely crazy about.** And they should not merely look good: **they should fit your feet perfectly, and be comfortable to walk in.** Want to know what happens to your feet if you spend too many years walking around in bad shoes or shoes that don't fit properly? Bunions, corns, shin splints . . . it's a long and very unattractive list. Do yourself a favor and use your head when you dress your feet!

The most important thing about shoes, however, is to have **fun** with them.

Don't get muddled down in all black—add some **color** to that shoe collection for your more playful moods. Learn about all the styles and materials shoes come in and **have a little shoe adventure.** The next page outlines some of the types of shoes out there.

Shoe Tree

Have you been trying to make sense of all the shoe types there are to choose from? Even a hip, well-heeled chick like you can sometimes be thrown for a loop when choosing the right shoe to complete your outfit, right? So to help you out, I've cobbled together a **list of some of the basics** that are shoo-ins (sorry) for fashion success!

Wedges.

The wedge heel has made a comeback, and good thing, since these are easy to walk in and are a great opportunity to get some extra height. From simple black wedge-heeled mules to the outrageous vinyl-and-lucite pair worn by **Pink** here, the funky heels work great with skirts or pants for a cool retro look.

Sandals.

A must for summer months, and holiday parties if it's not too chilly (no hose on those open toes, please!). Here, the **Mowry sisters** wear strappy high heels—the perfect way to show off twenty perfect toes!

Stilettos.

Here, **Liv Tyler** pairs classic stiletto mules with a pinstripe suit for a sexy look that's still all business. Don't bother wearing shoes like these if you find them hard to walk in—these skinny spikes may look dynamite, but the look quickly loses its charm if you can't walk tall and proud.

Platforms.

Super trendy, for the funkster chick who embraces the latest styles— **Drew Barrymore** is a big platform fan. Great with baggy pants and long skirts—and a quick way to grow a few inches for your date with the cute basketball player!

Boots.

Whether you wear them knee-high or more discreetly under pants, boots are always in style. And today you can find boots in all styles and lengths, from ultra-conservative to **Gwen Stefani**'s club-chic pair.

Cameron Diaz knew that long red beads would make the perfect adornment to this retro-style dotted floral dress. Black shoes and matching bag completed the look. To help block drafts—barely—she opted for a delicate wrap that matches her sky-blue eyes.

Finishing Touches

A finishing touch can make or break an outfit. The worst thing ever is when you've picked out the perfect dress, the perfect shoes, and the perfect jewelry—but the night you plan to wear them turns out colder than you thought it would. Hopefully, you have a shawl set aside for just an occasion, but if not…well, how weird does a ski jacket look with an evening gown! Take a few tips from these stars seem who have their finishing style down pat.

Tyra Banks added a gardenia to her gorgeous locks to complement her crystal earrings and matching crystal necklace.

Bai Ling complemented a bright blue, red-trimmed tank with a funky, multicolored bandanna in bright orange, yellow, and green.

Finally, we arrive at finishing touches—those little extras you add *to an* outfit that give it your final dose of style.

Pack It Away

Lisa Lopez of TLC opted for an evening-style backpack that matched her shoes to carry her stuff around at a recent event.

Tia and Tamara are huge Rugrats fans—evidenced by their choice of backpacks. They know that fun never has to be sacrificed for style.

Essentially, backpacks suit the carryall needs of your everyday life.

Brad Pitt's wife, **Jennifer Aniston**, spiced up a white formal sequined dress with a faux leopard skin purse.

Mena Suvari's elegant sparkling gown is accented by an equally sparkly evening bag.

Carry It Around

While you might not tote around a **handbag** or **pocketbook** on a daily basis, few things are more fun than **a stunning evening bag**.

Leelee Sobieski knows how to have a good time and make a statement all at once with her snakeskin-print suit and "alligator" purse.

Top It Off

While some people can really pull off a wide variety of sizes, styles, and colors when it comes to hats, **many of us are safer waiting until the weather gets cold** before we don one of these beauties. And don't forget: if you decide to wear a tight-fitting hat, you'd better be ready to wear it all day—or bring the right supplies to school with you to help you repoof. **Nothing says style emergency like hat head!**

Like her gal-pal Lil' Kim, **Mary J. Blige** loves outrageous outfits and never looks the same for two occasions. Here, she wears a crocheted cap of vibrant colors over shoulder-length-blonde hair.

Salma Hayek looks like a proper society lady off to tea with this charming garden hat finished off with a delightful ribbon flower.

Scarves—and I don't mean the ones you wear on a winter's day—can be used to **dress up** an outfit or **add a splash of color or pattern** to a tired old shirt or dress.

Wrap It Up

Your grandmother probably wouldn't crochet an outfit like this one for you: **Christina Aguilera** paired a multi-colored granny-style shawl with a black peek-a-boo crocheted skirt for the 1999 Teen Choice Awards.

Few people know how to accessorize as well as **Salma Hayek**. The bejeweled pewter-gray, cut velvet gown she wore to the 1999 VH-1 fashion awards (right) demanded something special to complement its elaborate detailing: a matching stole and rhinestone tiara did the job perfectly. But the simple, gold-trimmed cream dress she wore to the *Double Jeopardy* premiere (left) worked better with simpler accents: gold lamé sandals and purse, and a soft creamy pashmina around her bare shoulders.

Pashminas and shawls are great for **special occasions** when you want to wear a strapless number but the weather basically frowns on your choice.

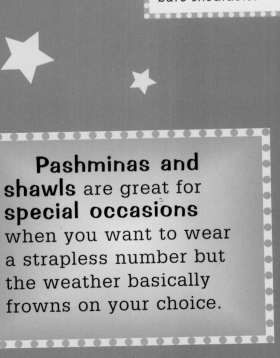

Resources

Books

Brous, Elizabeth, and the editors of *Seventeen. How To Be Gorgeous: The Ultimate Beauty Guide to Makeup, Hair, and More.* New York: HarperTrophy, 2000.
For girls who want to find the perfect look: tips on hair, makeup, skin care, nails, and more.

Brown, Bobbi, and Annemarie Iverson. *Teenage Beauty: Everything You Need to Look Pretty, Natural, Sexy & Awesome.* Cliff Street Books, 2000.
Makeup maven Bobbi Brown offers trade secrets and sensible advice to teens.

Chavez, Nick. *Perfect Hair Everyday.* QVC Publishing, 2000.
Let this Beverly Hills salon owner teach you the tricks to getting the salon look right in your own home.

Fekkai, Frederic. *A Year of Style.* New York: Clarkson Potter, 2000.
This stylist to the stars shares his tips in this month-by-month guide to simple beauty. Get information about clothing, accessories, mail polish, hair care products, makeup application, etc. Hundreds of photos!

Morley, Carol, and Liz Wild. *Hair: 100 Styling Secrets.* New York: Time Life, 2000.

Get tips from the pros on everything from banishing bad hair days to fighting the frizzies.

Morley, Carol, and Liz Wilde. *Faces: 100 Makeup Moves.* New York: Time Life, 2000.
A quick guide to choosing makeup, quick fixes, and the five-minute face.

Painell, Chrissie. *Over 100 Truly Astonishing Beauty Tips.* Carlton Books, 2000.

Tips on hair care, skin care, makeup, and perfume.

Magazines

Check out these magazines for the best beauty tips:

CosmoGirl	Glamour
Jane	Mademoiselle
Marie Claire	Seventeen
Sixteen	Teen People
YM	

Web Sites

Beautycare.com Lots of info about beauty here including weekly tips and an "Ask the Expert" message board.

Emakemeup.com This is an awesome website on beauty products. It includes reviews of tons of cosmetics, step-by-step application instructions, product suggestions, chat, and makeovers with before and after photos.

Pimpleportal.com One of my favorites by name alone! This site has everything you ever wanted to know about acne and then some, plus makeup tips and a question archive.

Profaces.com Have makeup questions? Ask here and they'll respond personally via email. This site also has tons of makeup tips and a free newsletter you can sign up for.

Punelive.com This site has beauty tips, Q & A, and even information on how to choose the right perfume.

Robertcraig.com This site is all about hair care. It features a tip of the week, a live chat with a stylist who will personally answer your questions via email, an on-line store, a free consultation, and more.

Salonweb.com This website has great information on hairstyles with lots of pictures and tips on hair care. Also many links.

Teenrefuge.com This is a great site that covers beauty, hair, fashion, and much more.

Clothing

Abercrombie & Fitch
www.abercrombie.com
1-800-432-0888

Aeropostale
www.aeropostale.com
email: webmaster
@aeropostale.com

Banana Republic
www.bananarepublic.com
1-888-906-2800

Blue Asphalt
www.blueasphalt.com
1-877-225-8327

Contempo Casuals
www.contempo-casuals.com
1-877-225-8327

dELiA*s
www.delias.com
1-877-333-5427

Express
www.expressfashion.com
email: talk
@expressfashion.com

Gap
www.gap.com
1-800-GAPSTYLE

Old Navy
www.oldnavy.com
1-800-OLD-NAVY

Wet Seal
www.wetseal.com
1-877-225-8327

Shoes & Accessories

Candies
www.candies.com
1-888-324-6356

Fornari USA
www.fornarina.com
323-782-1174

Nine West
www.ninewest.com
1-800-999-1877

Skechers
www.skechers.com
1-800-746-3411

Steve Madden
www.stevemadden.com
1-888-275-3633

Makeup and Skincare Products

BeautiControl Cosmetics
www.beauticontrol.com

Biore
www.biore.com
1-888-BIORE-11

Bonne Bell Cosmetics
www.bonnebell.com
1-800-537-1395

Buff Puff
www.mmm.com/bufpuf
1-800-537-1395

Cover Girl
www.covergirl.com

EyeLuv Cosmetics
www.eyeluv.com

M.A.C.
www.maccosmetics.com

Maybelline
www.maybelline.com

Neutrogena
www.neutrogena.com

Planet Pretty
www.planetpretty.com

Rock Candy
www.rock-candy.com
317-841-3535

Sephora
www.sephora.com

Stila
www.stilacosmetics.com
1-800-883-0400

Urban Decay Cosmetics
www.urbandecay.com

Wicked Colors
www.wickedcolors.com

Photo Credits

Archive Photos: ©Reuters/Rose Prouser: p. 32

London Features Int'l Ltd.: ©Gregg DeGuire: pp. 9; 29; 38 right; 57 right; 60; 61; 62; 65 left; 70 left; ©Anthony Dixon: pp. 5; 70 right; ©David Fisher: p. 83 top; ©Kevin Mazur: p. 44; ©Ilpo Musto: pp. 2; 78 right; ©Joy E. Scheller: p. 69 bottom; ©Dennis Van Tine: pp. 12; 20; 25 left; 45; 83 right; ©Ron Wolfson: pp. 39 right; 68 left

Retna Ltd.: ©Jenny Acheson: p. 58; ©Henry Arden/Camera Press: p. 27 top; ©Dana Belcher: p. 53 left; ©Capital Pictures: p. 71 top left; ©Capucine/Explorer: p. 31 left; ©Bill Davila: pp.11; 18; 35 left; 43 top; 63; 67 bottom right; 74; 79 right; 82 right; 89 left; ©Oscar Davis: p. 77 right; ©Robert Fairer: p. 52; ©Armando Gallo: pp. 21; 22–23; 25 right; 40 right; 42; 46 left; 47 left; 48; 49 left; 51 right; ©Ed Geller: pp. 65 top center; 85 right; ©Martin Godwin/Camera Press: p. 28; ©Steve Granitz: pp. 7; 13; 19; 24; 26; 27 bottom; 34; 35 right; 38 left; 39 left; 41; 49 right; 51 left; 53 right; 56 left; 57 left; 65 right; 66; 67 top right; 68 right; 69 top left; 71 bottom left; 71 right; 76 left; 76 right; 80; 82 left; 85 left; 86 left; 86 right; 87 bottom left; 87 right; 88; 89 right; 90; 91 left; ©Sam Levi: pp. 8; 47 right; ©Stewart Mark/ Camera Press: p. 16; ©Ernie Panniccioli: p. 77 left; ©Doug Peters/All Action: p. 83 left; ©John Ricard: p. 72; ©Sarie/Camera Press: p. 31 right; ©Paul Smith /FeatureFlash: pp. 50; 67 bottom left; 87 top left; ©John Spellman: pp. 10; 14; 40 left; 46 right; 54; 55; 56 right; 65 bottom center; 67 top left; 69 top right; 78 left; 84; 91 right; ©Richard Stonehouse/Camera Press: p. 30; ©Fabrice Trombert: pp. 1; 79 left; ©Scott Weiner: p. 43 bottom

Index